Cheers to the Gilmores

An Unofficial Gilmore Girls Themed Cocktail Book

J.L. McDermott

Copyright © 2025 by J. L. McDermott Hardcover Edition

All rights reserved. Not part of this publication may be reproduced or transmitted in any form or by any means, whether electronic, photocopying, videoing, or other means without prior written permission on writing from the author.

All inquiries should be addressed to: JLMcDermottbooks@gmail.com

Visit our socials at @j.l.mcdermott & @cheerstogilmores on TikTok & Instagram

Names: McDermott, J. L., author & photographer
Title: Cheers to the Gilmores, An Unofficial Gilmore Girls Themed Cocktail Book
Subjects: Cookbooks, Food & Wine › Celebrities & TV Shows
        Humor & Entertainment › Television › Shows

Cover design by J. L. McDermott
All cocktail photography by J.L. McDermott

ISBN 979-8-218-82560-7

Printed in the United States of America

This book is unofficial and unauthorized. It is not authorized, approved, licensed, or endorsed by Warner Bros Entertainment. Trademarks used in this book are property of their respective owners and are used for informational purposes only.

Dedication

To beautiful and nuanced relationships between mothers and daughters. To my own mothers, the one who raised me and the one who gave me life. And to my own daughter, who also lives in a world of books, I am so excited to read all of your future books.
I Love you ♥

To Amy Sherman-Palladino and all the cast and crew for creating and bringing this story to life, it has provided us the cozy comfort that generations have needed for literal decades, thank you.

Introduction

I love Gilmore Girls the way Lorelai loves snow and the way Rory loves books; I have since the very beginning and long before fall became the season to rewatch all our favorite episodes. I can't believe it has been 25 years. To write a book about something you and so many others love is a privilege but is also a little intimidating. So let me set a little bit of a roadmap. Firstly, if you have not seen the show, what are you even doing? Put this book down and go watch the show. For everyone else, let me state that even though this is a cocktail book, it is a Gilmore Girls book first. If you're a cocktail enthusiast, great, I hope you love this book! If you're a cocktail elitist, you may have come to the wrong place. This is meant to be a fun way to celebrate the show's beloved characters and themes while enjoying a tasty beverage.

Now for the cocktails: some of the cocktails in this book appear in the show while other cocktails are inspired by a character, a scene or a quote. All of them are meant to transport you and your Gilmore Girls loving friends to the world of Stars Hollow. I hope you enjoy experimenting with these recipes. Use them as a guide. I subscribe to the philosophy measure with your heart as we all have different tastes, especially when it comes to alcohol. I could probably write three more volumes of inspired recipes, but I poured my heart into these for so long that it is time for them to be out in the world. I hope you love them, and they inspire you to create your own! I will be publishing additional recipes on my social media page(s) which at this time is primarily TikTok. Follow us @ J.L.Mcdermott & Cheerstogilmores and we'd love to see you!

Cheers!

The Stars Hollow

Ah, Stars Hollow, and all of its cozy vibes. The town events that are unlike anywhere else make it the quirkiest small town that we wish existed. Since this is the setting where most of the magic happens, it of course needs its own themed cocktail. While Gilmore Girls is the ever constant background noise to my life, I know many fans of the show like to start their rewatch each fall; it certainly hits differently in the fall! So I hope that the ingredients listed below bring the magic of a fall season in Stars Hollow into your living rooms.

- 1 small mason jar
- 4 oz of favorite apple cider
- 2 oz of caramel vodka or bourbon
- Apple sliced finely for taste and garnish
- Cinnamon sticks to garnish (optional)
- Caramel drizzle (optional)
- Ice

- Add all wet ingredients to the shaker with ice and shake
- Fill glass halfway with fresh ice
- Pour cocktail, add garnishes & be transported to Stars Hollow.

*Option for a mule: Add 1.5 oz of ginger beer, 2 oz of cider, 2 oz of caramel vodka adjust measurements with your heart and use a mule glass

**Option for batch cocktail: Stir together 9oz of caramel vodka, 10 oz of cider, Chopped apples. Top off with ginger beer

Coffee Coffee Coffee

So much of the show takes place while drinking coffee at Luke's, so our second cocktail just had to be a coffee themed cocktail in honor of the diner we all love and all wish we could frequent. Maybe you have your very own "Luke's" in life, I hope you do. Fresh brewed coffee, coffee liquor, and coffee beans are the key ingredients for this cocktail. And while this technically would never appear on the menu at Luke's, we're going for the spirit of the thing with this one. We hope you put your phone down and love this Coffee Coffee Coffee cocktail!

- Martini glass
- Double shot of cooled Espresso
- ¾ oz Coffee Liquor
- 1.5 oz Vodka of choice
- 0.5 oz Simple Syrup
- 3 Coffee beans for an optional garnish

- Brew espresso and set aside to cool
- Fill a shaker with ice, cooled coffee, coffee liquor, simple syrup, and vodka and shake vigorously
- Strain into martini glass
- Garnish with coffee beans
- Get off your cell phone!

I Smell Snow

I smell snow. Did you hear it in Lorelai's voice? Lorelai and snow have a special relationship. Ok, sure the first snowfall, especially if it is just a light, pretty dusting- that feels magical. Snow around the holidays is also nice but as a New Englander who can get a little exhausted by snow, this particular magic escapes me. However, for Lorelai and the other snow lovers out there- this cocktail is for you, enjoy the magic! For those of us who cannot get behind snow, I think we can get behind the ingredients in this cocktail!

- Coupe glass (or martini glass)
- Simple syrup for rim
- Coconut flakes for garnish
- 3 oz Coconut Liquor
- 1.5 oz Coconut Rum
- ½ oz Simple Syrup
- Splash of lime juice
- 1 cup of ice

- Rim glass with simple syrup and dip in coconut flakes
- Add remainder of the ingredients to the cocktail shaker, shake well.
- Pour into coupe or martini glass
- Sprinkle coconut flakes on top for snow effect
- Share a magical relationship with snow! Do you smell it?

The Rory

The Rory is one of the few actual cocktails featured in the show so of course had to be included. The Rory brings us on a bit of a martini streak, but we couldn't have a Lorelai cocktail without a Rory one immediately following. Lorelai would tell you that this is not a martini anyway. The Rory is going to be too sweet for some and possibly delightful for others. What can we say about this drink other than it is pink, very pink and it's meant to be drunk as though it is your special day, so cheers to you! Pinkies up. Drink like you're 21 again! (Ok, maybe don't do that.)

- Martini glass
- 2oz of pineapple vodka, chilled
- 4oz of Champagne or Perseco
- Splash of Grenadine
- Coarse granulated sugar colored pink with food coloring for rim
- Fresh pineapple or simple syrup for rim

- Rim glass with pineapple & sugar
- In shaker, shake vodka and grenadine
- Top with Champagne or Perseco

Kim's Antiques

Lane and Mrs. Kim both add so much to the show mainly by being so uniquely different! As Seventh Day Adventists (at least Lane in the early seasons), it is only fitting that we include a mocktail. This drink is perfect for dry January, for hosting non drinking friends or for any moment when you just want the refreshing feeling of a fancy seltzer. Inspired by all of the tea and health foods that Mrs. Kim makes for Lane this is a Honey, Lemon, Ginger Fizzy Mocktail. The ginger is fiery like Mrs. Kim's personality!

- Goblet
- 1.5 oz fresh squeezed lemon juice
- Honey to taste
- Ginger to taste
- Favorite seltzer or sparkling water
- Lemon slices for garnish

- Fill goblet with ice
- Pour in lemon juice, honey, ginger and top with sparkling water
- Stir
- Garnish with lemon slices

Donna Reed Jello Shots

This drink, as I'm sure you guessed, is for Dean and is inspired by the Donna Reed episode. Some people hate on this episode, but I appreciate what Rory was trying to do here whether it hit right or not. I agree that it does feel a bit like a fever dream. I think even if you are a Dean hater, you have to agree that the beginning of Rory and Dean's relationship was super sweet. They represent high school relationship goals in many ways. And can I just say that I want that peach dress for a 1950s style photo shoot please? A cornstarch cocktail would have been challenging to pull off so here we are.

- 6 oz of lime Jello
- 1 cup of boiled water
- 1 cup of tequila
- 1 cup of margarita mix

- Add Jello to a bowl
- Add hot water and stir for 2 minutes
- Add tequila, margarita mix, and a pinch of salt
- Pour into containers and chill for at least 4 hours
- Garnish with whipped cream

For Fez

I love the relationship that Rory and her grandfather share throughout the show. We see this side of Richard at times with Emily and in a few rare moments with Lorelai, but he is consistently softer and more connected with Rory. The two share a unique bond from the beginning and it evolves throughout the series. I wanted to name this cocktail For Fez after that sweet conspiratorial moment where Richard hands Rory an envelope filled with money and says that it is "for Fez" after she had shared that dream trip with him. If you're on social media you've likely heard the audio: "So what's the verdict?" to which he replies " I am an autumn." This honestly nails it on the head. She handed him a Cosmo magazine and he not only read it but he took one of the quizzes. He is different with Rory and I'm here for it. I think the obvious choice for Richard is an Old Fashioned. Rest in peace, Edward Herman.

-1 Sugar cube
-2-3 dashes of Angostura bitters
-1 teaspoon of water
-2 oz of Bourbon or Rye Whiskey
-Orange twist for garnish
-Maraschino cherry
-Ice

-Place sugar cube in a chilled rocks glass
-A bitters directly onto the cube followed by the water
-Muddle together until a paste is formed
-Add a large ice cube to the glass
-Pour Bourbon or Rye Whiskey over the ice
-Stir the mixture for about 20-30 seconds until chilled
-To garnish, Express oil from orange peel over the glass and then drop it into the drink and add a cherry

Buy Me a Boa

Whether you love Emily or think she is the worst, you can't deny that she is an incredibly rich character who adds a lot to the show. The daily life of Emily Gilmore may seem to consist of planning perfect high society events, attending DAR meetings, firing maids, and casting judgment on her daughter, but I love that we get to see more of Emily in the later seasons. Her one liners are everything and Kelly Bishop is an absolute queen. The Buy Me a Boa cocktail is not two glasses of wine but a gimlet you would perhaps enjoy even more in pearls.

-1 oz of lime juice
-1 oz simple syrup
-2 oz of Vodka
-Lime for garnish

-Add wet ingredients into a shaker
-Add ice & shake
-Strain into a coupe glass
-Garnish with a Lime

Call Me Ace

Whether you're Team Logan or not, I hope you'll love this cocktail. Logan is pure charisma incarnated. He has boyish charm and the old money doesn't hurt. Do not even get me started with The Life and Death Brigade since those are some of my favorite episodes. Most importantly, he shows up when it matters, he has a deep love for Rory and he tried to be the boyfriend he thought she wanted until other forces (particularly Mitchum) had to mess a lot up for these two. Who knows what could have been? Let's raise a glass to what ifs with this very fitting Goldrush cocktail.

- 2 oz of Bourbon
- 1 oz Lemon juice
- ¾ oz Honey syrup

- Shake over ice
- Double strain over ice
- Express lemon over glass and garnish

Oy with the Poodles Already

This may be one of the most popular {and nonsensical} Lorelai quotes. I love a good Lorelai quote, rant, or monologue especially punctuated by some spot on sarcasm. Lorelai's spunky spirit as both a reaction to and a celebration of the town she comes from is probably what resonates with viewers no matter what generation they belong to. Enjoy this Oy with the Poodles Already Cocktail with the favorite sarcastic sidekicks in your life.

- 2 oz of Vanilla Vodka
- 2 oz of Coconut Rum
- 2 z of Half and Half
- Splash of Coconut Cream

- Shake in a shaker
- Pour into a martini glass
- Garnish with marshmallows

The Rude Frenchman

Do we love him, do we hate him? Would he drink this? This drink probably has too many calories for him but perhaps if his mother was visiting. Michel is a lot, but his personality does add something different to balance the sweetness and quirkiness that Sookie brings. He certainly has some good one liners. And ultimately, I think we know he has Lorelai's back. What better cocktail for Michel than the classic cocktail, a French 75?

- 1.5 oz of Gin
- 0.5 oz of Fresh Lemon Juice
- 0.5 oz Simple Syrup
- Champagne/Sparkling Wine

- Shake
- Strain into a Champagne Flute
- Top with Sparkling Wine
- Garnish with a lemon

The Puffs

This Chilton secret society may have a fluffy sounding name, but they didn't mess around. The initiation by hazing ritual of breaking into the school and headmaster's office is pretty serious though ringing a bell certainly isn't high crime. And their chant could use some work. Francie certainly gave Paris some competition though. But let's face it, the name is giving pink and poofy vibes and so shall the drink.

- Martini glass
- Forsting or Marshmallow
- Pink Sprinkles
- Rose Sparkling Wine

- Rim glass with frosting or marshmallow & sprinkles
- Add pink cotton candy to glass
- Pour Rose Sparkling wine

Why did you drop out of Yale?!!

This cocktail is for the Jess fans. Jess entered the show like a whirlwind, poor Pierpont. Despite this, it is easy to see why Team Jess sees Jess as the end game for Rory. What I love about Jess is not only how he truly sees Rory but the hidden depth to his character; he comes across as the bad boy when he is an intelligent and truly insightful person. In fairness, stealing garden gnomes and skipping school to work isn't exactly the road to a hardened life of crime. Jess is the one who got her to go back to school when she was so lost. I don't think he was the best boyfriend to Rory but I do think we see the most growth from his character. Seeing grown up Jess at the end of A Year in The Life standing on Lorelai's porch and the way he looks at her really makes me want more episodes!

- Highball glass
- Ice
- ½ a lime
- Ginger beer of choice
- 2 oz Rum

- Fill glass with ice
- Squeeze juice from 1/2 lime into glass & save husk for garnish
- Fill glass ¾ full with ginger beer
- Drizzle Rum on top slowly so it layers
- Add lime husk to garnish

Norman Mailer, I'm Pregnant

This is classic Sookie. Lorelai and Sookie have opened the Dragonfly Inn and their dream has become reality when they have someone famous visiting. Just one problem, he won't order any food no matter how hard Sookie tries. I love the quirky way Snookie confronts Mailer for only ordering iced tea only to later find out that it was a pregnancy hormone driven rant.

- 6-8 oz of your favorite black, green, or fruit tea brewed and cooled
- 2 oz of bourbon
- 1 oz of lemon juice
- ½ oz of simple syrup
- Drizzle of honey
- Handful of raspberries
- Raspberries for garnish
- Ice

- Muddle raspberries with simple syrup & honey
- Add wet ingredients to a shaker
- Shake vigorously

To serve:
Fill glass with ice
Pour raspberry bourbon iced tea

The "Lor"

The "Lor" cocktail is of course inspired by Christopher. My apologies to any Christopher fans out there but after my - I don't know how many -eth rewatches of the series, my tolerance for Christopher and his absentee parenting is basically non-existent. Does anyone else get the ick when he calls Lorelai that?

They did have their moments. The chemistry was undeniable at times, but the ways in which he did not show up for either of them is pretty terrible. To miss your one and only daughter's graduation is next level absentee parenting. The inspiration for this cocktail is the episode where Lorelai and Chris go to Yale for Parents Weekend, and Christopher insists on taking the staff of the Yale Daily News out to dinner. He orders a round of cognac and creme brulee for the table, but Rory and the rest of the paper staff get called away leaving it all uneaten. Christopher is caught trying to overcompensate for all the times he was not around for Rory, and I must admit I did not hate this one bit.

- 1 oz Cognac
- 1 oz Amaretto
- 1 oz Vanilla syrup
- ¾ oz Milk
- 1.5 oz Cream
- Granulated sugar for garnish
- Creme Brulee torch

- Combine wet ingredients in shaker & shake
- Pour into coupe glass or martini glass
- Sprinkle granulated sugar over top
- Use Creme Brulee torch to create caramelized garnish

Founders' Day Punch

Founders' Day Punch is a must for a cocktail book due to the iconic scene where it's described for its ability to remove tar. This ability tracks when considering its maker Miss Patty never holds back with her gossip that packs a punch either. It's first mentioned at the Firelight Festival and appears to be the drink of Taylor and Miss Patty while judging the dance-a-thon. And who can forget its presence when Paris comes to town for the opening of the Twickham Museum?

-Mason jar
-1 oz light rum
-1oz dark rum
-5 oz of your favorite juice cocktail (this was Miss Patty & the early 2000s, this is what we're doing)

-Add ingredients to shaker
-Shake vigorously
-Pour over Mason jar filled with ice
-Garnish as desired: Cherries, orange, lemon, whatever you have on hand

One Thousand Yellow Daisies

You have to hand it to Max Medina, he certainly had a way with words and grand gestures (though one could argue it was from so much time spent studying the literary masterpieces.) I really liked Max as a person and thought he was a genuine guy despite overstepping some boundaries to date the parent of a student. Does one thousand yellow daisies match your idea of the perfect proposal? Whether you're into grand gestures or something a little more subtle, hopefully you'll find this daisy style cocktail is spot on for you.

- Daisy glass
- 2 oz of your favorite gin
- ½ oz of cointreau
- 1 oz of lemon juice
- 1 oz of grenadine
- Ice

- Pour ingredients into shaker & shake
- Pour into daisy glass until half full
- Top with soda water
- Garnish with daisies

*please only use clean, pesticide-free daisies that are food safe

It should have been Rygalski

Of all the ways in which Lane was robbed on the show, this was perhaps the biggest. We have to wonder what would have happened with their storyline had Adam Brody not been cast on the OC. Sigh. Some argue Dave Rygalski is better than all the Gilmore Girls boyfriends combined. I mean, he did take on Mrs. Kim. He read the entire bible for Lane and showed up for her in so many ways. When trying to think of a cocktail to represent Dave, I needed something wholesome. What's more wholesome than a chocolate chip cookie?

-Glass
-1.5 oz Vanilla Vodka
-1.5 oz Rumchata
-1.5 oz Chocolate Liquor
-1TBS Chocolate Sauce
-Whipped Cream
-Sprinkles
-Mini Chocolate Chip Cookie for garnish

-Combine wet ingredients into shaker with ice & shake
-Pour into glass
-Garnish with whipped cream, sprinkles, & cookie

Sleeping with the Zucchini

Don't worry it's not an actual Zucchini cocktail, I took some liberties here (although perhaps someone with a vision could create something masterful with zucchini.) This cocktail is for Jackson and I substituted zucchini with some deliciously refreshing cucumber slices. The dedication Jackson puts into his farming and the care he puts into each and every vegetable is only matched by his commitment to his relationship with Sookie. He is passionate about what he does, and I enjoy the banter that he and Sookie have throughout the show. I love the episode where he sleeps with the zucchini to make sure the crop does not freeze ahead of the opening of the inn.

- 3 cucumber slices
- 1.5 oz of Gin
- 0.5 oz Simple Syrup
- 1 oz Lemon Juice

- Muddle cucumber slices
- Add wet ingredients to shaker
- Shake with Ice
- Double strain into a cocktail glass
- Garnish with cucumber rolls

Monkey Monkey Underpants

Well, actually hockey puck, rattlesnake, monkey monkey, underpants. But of course, you knew that. Lorelai is still with Christopher {sigh} while trying to be a good friend to Luke by writing him a character reference letter. Shocker, she is having a hard time doing so. And we all know how that ends up. If you don't, put this book down right now and stop sleeping on Gilmore Girls. What are you even doing with your life? Out of this episode was born a classic Lorelai Gilmore monologue, one that has been quoted for two decades. Therefore, we had to make a Monkey Monkey Underpants inspired cocktail. Or is it an ode to Lorelai and Luke's unwavering connection? Either way, I hope you're here for it!

1.5 oz of Jamaican Rum
1 oz banana liqueur
½ oz Burnt sugar syrup
2 oz of coconut milk
½ oz orgeat

Combine wet ingredients in a shaker
Add ice
Shake well
Pour into a high ball glass
Garnish with banana or toasted marshmallow

Picklegate

This cocktail is less in honor of the train that derailed carrying 3.5 tons of pickles, causing an unbearable stench throughout Stars Hollow and more in honor of the infamous town meetings, and Taylor being Taylor. Also, you may remember a different episode where Sookie and Jackson are running through the town with trash bags full of "pickles," I mean marijuana, that Jackson somehow accidentally grew. This author also loves pickles, so behold The Picklegate Cocktail!

1.5 oz of pickle juice
2 oz of your favorite Vodka
Splash of Vermouth
Coupe glass
Small gherkins to garnish

Combine wet ingredients in a shaker with ice
Shake shake shake
Pour into glass
Garnish with gherkins

A Drink by Kirk

I wanted to name this drink Babette Ate Oatmeal, but an oatmeal cookie shot is not the best fit for Kirk's character. So after A Film by Kirk seemed like the next best option. Kirk is arguably the most random character on the show, but who doesn't love Kirk? As he is the man of many jobs, I think a flight is in order. Furthermore, he is kind of like a child in a lot of ways, so I thought boozy sodas would also be fitting.

1) -½ oz Grenadine
-1 ½ oz Vodka
-Favorite Lemon Lime Soda
-Add ice to glass
-Add maraschino cherries & Grenadine
-Fill glass slightly more than halfway with soda
-Add Vodka

2) -1 ½ oz of Whipped Vodka
-Favorite orange soda
-Splash of vanilla creamer
-Add ice to glass
-Add vodka
-Fill most of the way with soda
-Add a splash of creamer

3) -1 ½ oz of Vanilla Vodka
-Favorite Rootbeer
-Scoop of Vanilla Ice Cream
-Add ice to glass
-Add vodka
-Fill most of the way with soda
-Top with ice cream (or whipped cream)

In Omnia Paratus

"You Jump, I Jump, Jack" has to be one of my favorite episodes. Whether you're team Logan or not, I think you have to admit that they had some tremendous chemistry. I love so many of the lines from this episode: "It's a once in a lifetime experience" and the response "Only if you want it to be." Do they even make men like this? In Omnia Paratus. Prepared for anything. This episode is everything.

- 2 oz Empress Gin
- 1 oz Fresh Lemon
- 1 oz Simple Syrup
- Champagne

- Add ice to shaker
- Add all ingredients {except champagne}
- Shake
- Strain into glass with ice
- Top with champagne & stir
- Garnish with a lemon & a black umbrella

The Paris Geller

It was tricky coming up with a fitting cocktail for Paris. We love a rich character, and Paris nails rich to a tee. I actually enjoy watching her character develop and her relationship with Rory evolve over the course of the series. From trying to be number one at Chilton, to crashing out during the Harvard application process and again while editor of the Yale Daily News, to connecting more authentically with Rory. Her storylines trigger a lot of secondhand embarrassment but I could never hate this queen.

- Tajin
- ¼ Cup of Lime juice
- 2 oz Favorite Tequila
- Agave
- 1 oz Cointreau
- 4 slices of jalapeno

- Use lime to rim glass
- Add Tajin to rim of glass
- Add a 3 jalapeno slices & a small amount of agave to shaker and muddle
- Add in tequila, cointreau, lime juice, and ice to shaker
- Shake well
- Pour into glass and garnish with a jalapeno

The Vicious Trollop

This cocktail needed to be included, since it references one of my favorite Emily and Lorelai scenes. I am not a red lipstick girl, but this could possibly convert me. Vicious Trollop is iconic. And more than that, it symbolizes those rare moments when Emily and Lorelai can bond. Mother and daughter getting along despite everything. Pudding anyone?

- 1 ½ oz Favorite Tequila
- ½ oz Simple Syrup
- ½ oz Triple Sec
- ½ oz Lime Juice
- 1 oz Pomegranate Juice

- Combine ingredients in shaker
- Add ice
- Shake well
- Strain into a martini glass

The Dragonfly

The Dragonfly is more than an inn, it is a dream. Two friends chasing their dream and achieving it. Sure, Lorelai having extremely wealthy parents who helped her out along the way did not hurt, but I think with her tenacity she would have found a way regardless. I love that her friends stayed for the soft launch. I also love that the community rallies around her because she's truly built a home and a community in Stars Hollow.

- 2oz of Lemonade
- ¾ oz of Dragonfruit Syrup
- 1oz of Soda Water
- 1.5oz of Empress Gin

- Fill glass with ice
- Add ingredients to glass in order listed to create layered effect
- The acid in the lemonade will change the color in the gin, you can also use peaflower powder with another type of gin for the same effect

The Hep Alien

This cocktail is for our favorite Korean rocker girl. How can you not love her progression from squirrelling away CDs in the floorboards of her bedroom to actualizing her lifelong dream of being a drummer in a rock band? Even though she rails against her Seventh Day Adventist roots, she's still not a drinker, so I think a mocktail is the perfect choice. And also, there was the episode where she got completely drunk off of ½ a beer; so again, mocktail. A beverage in a lovely shade of purple as an homage to the dyed bright purple hair that she had for 3.5 seconds was a consideration, but this particular beverage is refreshing and the shade is giving alien.

- One fourth of a honey dew melon, cubed
- 2 oz of lime juice
- 1 oz simple syrup
- Seltzer

- Blend melon, syrup, and lime juice
- Strain into shaker
- Add ice and and top with seltzer and shake
- Add to a glass of ice and cubed melon

The Floaty Hut

Yes, I know, y'all have a lot to say about A Year In The Life. I have feelings about it too, but it was funny to see Luke, the curmudgeon, be so protective of his floaty hut. And also, Stars Hollow has a pool? Yes, there is some cringe to this episode (I don't really love the whole part where Lorelai and Rory are sitting poolside and being fanned) but as a Gilmore Girls fan, give me all the Gilmore Girls all the time, in fact, it's time for more! Something I really enjoyed about AYITL was seeing the characters in different elements, I think the mini movies were fun that way. There was so much time spent in the pool house during the regular series but never in the pool and this cocktail is definitely not something the Gilmores would serve. This cocktail has all the vibes of summer.

- Popsicle
- Sliced strawberries
- 1-2 oz of your favorite Vodka
- Lemonade

- Add ice to bottom of glass
- Add Vodka
- Fill glass most of the way with Lemonage
- Add popsicle and sliced strawberries

The Pro Con List

Rory is the queen of the Pros and Cons list so this cocktail is quite possibly more fitting than 'The Rory". She made pros and cons lists for absolutely everything: deciding between Harvard and Yale, making boyfriend decisions, and choosing what newspaper she wanted to work for. She also made lots of lists in general throughout the series. The major ingredient of this cocktail captures another personality trait of Rory's (and Lorelai's): the love of Poptarts™. I am not sure how many times Poptarts™ are mentioned throughout the series, but it is a lot.

- Rocks glass
- Mini Poptarts™ for garnish
- A few fresh strawberries
- 1.5 oz of Simple Syrup
- 1.5 oz of Vanilla Vodka
- 1.5 oz of White Chocolate Liquor
- Pinch of salt

- Muddle a handful of strawberries in a shaker with simple syrup
- Add liquid ingredients and shake
- Pour into cocktail glass over ice
- Garnish with whipped cream, a whole strawberry and a mini Poptart™

Friday Night Dinner

Friday night dinners are one of the constants throughout the show, so, of course, we had to create a Friday Night Dinner cocktail. These scenes are filled with banter, a revolving door of maids, Emily's one liners, endless family drama, and of course cocktails. During one such dinner, Emily passive aggressively says, "I could have sworn you were a sidecar girl" to Lorelai whose drink most Fridays is a martini. This encapsulates so much of the spirit of things, don't you think? So the Friday night dinner is a sidecar cocktail.

-Chilled Coupe or Nick and Nora Glass
-Lemon
-Sugar
-2 oz of Cognac
-1 oz of Cointreau
-½ oz of Lemon juice

-Rim chilled glass with sugar
-Combine wet ingredients in a shaker with ice
-Express lemon over the glass
-Pour cocktail into the glass & garnish

Nitwit Juice

This is a great episode and it's also a fun name for a drink. Emily continuously throwing veiled insults such as calling the diner "rustic" and offering Luke a "beeeer" in her specific way that is insulting without actually saying anything insulting is honestly an art form. A lot can be said about Emily, but that character is written so well and Kelly Bishop plays it brilliantly. Luke wasn't much of a drinker, but let's be honest, if given a well-stocked bar, he'd likely choose a beer. He is a no frills, flannel wearing, what you see is what you get kind of a guy which is refreshing after seeing Lorelai endure Christopher, Digger, and yes, even Max. We turned Nitwit Juice into a cocktail, and we hope you enjoy it!

-Chilled Pilsner glass
-Equal parts cold light beer and lemonade
-Garnish with lemon wheel

Hey Mary

You may have guessed that this next cocktail is named after Tristan. Social media has introduced me to some surprising truths about life out in the world. One truth that surprised me is that Team Tristan is a thing and even more surprising is how many members there appear to be on his team. So this one is for all of you. If Tristan was not a high schooler, an obvious choice would be a Bloody Mary; but since he was only around during the Chilton years, let's go in a completely different direction. I could see our boy being a fan of energy drinks, especially with their newness in the early 2000s, so whether you get the Tristan hype or not, we hope you'll enjoy this fun dirty energy drink!

-Glass filled with ice
-Fill most of the way with your favorite energy drink
-Add 2 pumps of a complimenting flavored syrup (i.e. cherry drink and cherry or vanilla syrup)
-Top with a generous splash of creamer

The Troubador

The town troubadour is honestly just classic Stars Hollow. It's often a silly story element, adding either some lighthearted humor or some conflict with Taylor. Chill vibes are in order to embody this character so something similar to a pina colada is fitting.

-Ice
-1.5 oz of White Rum
-3 oz of Cream of Coconut
-6 oz of Pineapple Juice
-Cherry to garnish

-Add ingredients to a shaker or a blender- this drink can be enjoyed both ways
-Blend until desired consistency and add to a hurricane glass
-For non blended option, stir ingredients then add to glass
-Garnish with a cherry
-As a variation, add a slash of grenadine for a delicious pink pina colada

The Secret Bar

I absolutely love the vibe of a speakeasy and their popularity appears to be growing. But what I love about The Secret Bar, apart from subverting Taylor, is that it is an aspect introduced in A Year In The Life that feels like it could have always been there. I went back and forth a little on what cocktail I wanted to feature here. Lorelai orders a gin martini with a twist and Michel orders a shot of tequila in the scene, but I thought it to be befitting to do something a la the prohibition era. I LOVE how they yell five-o when Taylor approaches and hide!

-Chilled coupe glass
-2 oz of Bourbon
-1 oz of Sweet Vermouth
-2 dashes of Angostura Bitters
-1 Maraschino cherry for garnish

-Add Bourbon, Vermouth, and Bitters to a mixing glass
-Fill the glass with ice
-Stir until the outside of the glass is well chilled
-Strain into a chilled coupe glass
-Garnish with cherry

Cinnamon's Wake

If you haven't guessed, this cocktail is for Babette and Morey. Babette and Morey are two more beloved Stars Hollow characters and they adored their cat, Cinnamon. When I asked on social media what was the worst drink of the early 2000s, the resounding response was all of the cinnamon liquors...I feel like we need a cinnamon cocktail because they were so prominent in this time period but understand that mixed with the right ingredients, a cinnamon cocktail can hit just right. I would not want to hear Babette's voice after a few of these though.

- Rocks glass
- Ice
- Cinnamon Whiskey
- Pinapple Juice
- Orange Soda
- Cherry

- Fill rocks glass with ice
- Add Cinnamon Whiskey about ⅓ of the way or to preference
- Add Pineapple Juice leaving a little room for soda
- Top with Orange Soda
- Garnish with a cherry

The Fun Flask

"Bulldog, bulldog bow-wow-wow Eli Yale!" It was fun to see Richard in his element tailgating at the Harvard/Yale game and the fun flask is something different and outside of the usual cocktail cart. We don't know exactly what was in the fun flask, so really the sky is the limit here. You can choose to serve this in a fancy leather bound flask like Richard, or a pink and sparkly flask like mine that is definitely Lorelai approved. Either way, embrace the care free spirit of Richard (here) as you sip on this!

- 1 oz Vodka
- ½ oz Blue Curacao
- Lime wedge

- Add wet ingredients to a shaker with ice
- Shake only long enough to chill shot but not water it down
- Strain into flask or shot glass
- Squeeze lime over top

The Funky Monkey

When Rory and Paris are moving out of their dorm freshman year, everyone on the floor has poured their leftover alcohol together to create the Funky Monkey. The obvious reaction to this scene should be: BAD IDEA. But I decided to try it out and believe it or not... it's not too bad. Give it a try after you host a Gilmore Girls party serving a selection of these cocktails, and you just don't want those leftovers to go to waste!

-Pint glass filled with ice or Red Solo™ cup for effect
-Add a small splash of a variety of 5-6 liquors to glass
-Top with lemon lime soda
-There is no garnish here, this is a college dorm leftover cocktail, but if you must, you must

Who's My Daddy?

This cocktail is after the ever controversial April Nardini. My take, she was a child. Anna, on the other hand... well, on to the cocktail. This cocktail gets its name from April's Science Fair project. It is a Capri Sun™ based cocktail because April offers Luke one when he is a little shocked at the news. I also learned that you can put a small slit into the pouch, add alcohol and then close up the slit with a hair straightener. **Please do this responsibly and do not store or keep where a child could mistake this for a juice box!

-Capri Sun™ of choice, let freeze 5-6 hours minimum
-Leave out to defrost for a little bit to create a nice slush, about 30 minutes
-Add small slit in pouch
-1oz favorite Vodka, Rum, or Tequilla
-Squeeze of lime

Gypsy's Lemonade

This cocktail is inspired both by the character of Gypsy herself and also the Hay Bale Maze episode. Sadly, the budget for Gypsy's lemonade booth at the Spring Fling was misappropriated by none other than Taylor Doose. I love Gypsy's no nonsense character resulting in the need for a refreshing cocktail to embody her spirit. Perhaps enjoy it with some salty nuts.

- 32oz Mason jar
- 2 large lemons
- ¼ cup of sugar
- 1 cup of ice
- 2oz Vodka
- 2 cups of water

- Slice lemon into 6 slices
- Add lemon and sugar to your cocktail shaker and muddle well
- Add ice, vodka, and water and shake everything together
- Pour into mason jar
- Garnish with additional lemon slices

I'm in, I am all in

We could not let this book exist without a cocktail named after this iconic line from Luke. I love everything about this scene, from Luke having his own "Luke's" to the horoscope that he kept in his wallet for 8 years. And, of course, telling Lorelai that he is all in- is everything. While I don't really think we need another champagne cocktail, it is what they drank in the scene.

-2 oz of your favorite Vodka
-Juice of ½ a lime
-Little sugar
-Champagne

-Add vodka, lime juice, sugar, and ice to shaker
-Give a good shake
-Pour into a Coupe
-Top with Champagne
-Garnish with a lime

www.ingramcontent.com/pod-product-compliance
Lightning Source LLC
Chambersburg PA
CBHW060054070526
44107CB00162B/670